ALL PRE...

By the same author:
  Battle Stations
  Believing is Seeing

All Preachers Great and Small

PETER GAMMONS

Cartoons by
DREW NORTHCOTT

MINSTREL
Eastbourne

Cartoons by Drew Northcott
Cover design by W James Hammond

British Library Cataloguing in Publication Data
Gammons, Peter
All preachers great and small.
I. Title
828'.91407

ISBN 1-85424-020-X

Printed in Great Britain for
Minstrel, an imprint of Monarch Publications Ltd
1 St Anne's Road, Eastbourne, E Sussex BN21 3UN by
Richard Clay Ltd, Bungay, Suffolk.
Typeset by Nuprint Ltd, 30b Station Road, Harpenden,
Herts AL5 4SE.

Dedication

To all the 'victims' whose stories are contained herein, without whom this book would have been boring.

Also to Mum and Dad, without whose initial help this book would have been greatly hindered.

Contents

Foreword

Laughter is good for all of us—and nothing is funnier than the truth. Our God is a God of truth and laughter, and also of great joy.

I really enjoyed these stories that Peter Gammons has collected. They should give a lot of pleasure to a lot of people, and I am very pleased to commend them to you.

Dana
April 1989

Acknowledgements

Thanks to Dave, Derek, Yvonne and Carolyn for their help in completing this book (and for numerous cups of coffee). Also to Ian and Rita for their support.

Many thanks to all those who have sent in contributions.

Prologue

Some time ago a man was commissioned to take a traffic survey at a busy intersection in one of America's major cities. He noted that people were thoroughly enjoying themselves and one another as they walked to church on Sunday mornings. However, they suddenly became rigid, formal, sober and quiet as they approached the door of the church.

At the conclusion of the service they came out of the building very piously and that was how they remained until they had crossed the street, when they seemed to relax, talk and become 'normal' again.

One of the man's questions at the end of his task was, 'What goes on in churches to deprive people of all joy?'

So for those who associate Christianity with propriety and sobriety, I trust *All Preachers Great and Small* will be a real eye-opener, and that you will have as much fun reading it as I have had compiling it.

Peter Gammons

'A cheerful heart is good medicine.'
Proverbs 17:22

1

Bizarre Blessings

The American Talking Clock Corporation has taken things to the limit. 'The Last Supper Talking Clock' has a digital display in the middle of the table, and a different disciple announces the time each hour, followed by soft music.

Never alone

A North London woman, charged with driving unaccompanied and without L plates, denied the allegation, claiming to be a Christian.

Appearing before Hendon magistrates, she said, 'I know it was Christ who guided me. He was sitting in the car supervising me.'

Although her instructor was invisible, his presence could not be doubted, she went on to explain.

Neighbours

A launderette and a religious bookshop in Sydney, Australia, have agreed a joint name for their adjoining premises. They have called it: 'Cleanliness is next to Godliness'.

Everything must go

Miss Winifred Mosen was surprised when the church caretaker asked her for the return of an old cardigan which she had purchased at the jumble sale to unpick for wool. It turned out that the lady on that particular stall had sold all the caretaker's washing!

Just in time

Accounts of people who have forgotten to put their clocks back an hour and arrived at a service just in time for the last hymn are not difficult to find. However, it is always amusing (or embarrassing) when the clergyman arrives late.

One notable account concerned a visiting preacher who arrived after the service had started. He dashed straight into the pulpit as the congregation finished a hymn and immediately launched into his sermon.

When he walked to the door after the final hymn to shake hands with people as they left, he was stopped by a minister in a clerical collar, who said 'Thank you for your message this morning. We really enjoyed it. However, we were not expecting you. Who are you?'

At this point he realised that he had gone to the wrong church.

No love lost

The relationship between a young curate and his vicar was rather strained, to say the least, and on his final Sunday before moving to a new church he chose as his text 'Tarry ye here with the ass while I go yonder'.

007

In Toronto, Canada, there is a church called St James Bond United Church.

Stop bugging me

A paranoid minister who had smuggled Bibles into
Russia was convinced that his hotel room had been
bugged. Rolling back the carpet in a thorough
search of his room, he found a brass bolt which he
assumed was the bugging device. As he set to
unscrewing it, the chandelier in the entrance hall
crashed to the ground.

Well heard

Cirencester Parish Church is very beautiful, and also
rather large. When Captain Woodhouse of the
Church Army arrived to preach there, the vicar
informed him: 'Captain, you have to speak up as
our loudspeaker system is not working.'

'I always try to ensure that everybody hears me,'
Captain Woodhouse replied.

At the end of the service, as he stood with the
vicar to say goodbye to everyone, a rather elderly
retired clergyman came up to them. 'I've told you
before, vicar,' he said 'but the loudspeaker system
was too loud again this morning.'

What a catastrophe

After his cat had got stuck in a tree, a pastor from
South Africa mounted a rescue operation. He
climbed a ladder as far as he could, tied one end of
a rope to the narrow trunk, and then tied the other
end to his car bumper. As he drove forward, inten-

ding to bring the bough down far enough for the cat to jump off, the inevitable happened—the rope broke, catapulting the moggy into space. No more was heard of the poor creature until a couple of weeks later. The pastor was in the supermarket when he saw one of his church members buying cat food. 'I didn't know you had a cat', he said enquiringly.

'I didn't. It's a funny story, quite a miracle really. About two weeks ago I was having a picnic on the lawn with my daughter. "I'd like to have a cat, Mummy," she said. "You'll have to ask Jesus for one," I replied. At that very moment this cat came flying through the air and landed on the lawn, and he's stayed with us ever since.'

An explosive situation

One well known evangelist put his briefcase down while he unlocked his car. He drove off, leaving the case in the hotel car park.

Imagine his embarrassment later that day when the police turned up with his case, and he learned that the area had been evacuated and the bomb squad called out to dismantle it. The contents were a New Testament, an apple and a packet of sandwiches.

Your sins will find you out

A travelling preacher was put up in a small cottage which had been built so that one had to pass through the other bedrooms to get to the bathroom. He noticed a chamber pot strategically placed in his room in case of emergencies.

During the night he needed to use the aforementioned item. In the morning he was too embarrassed to walk through the adjacent rooms with it, so he opened the windows and poured the contents out. But to his dismay the handle came loose and the porcelain utensil crashed to the path below at the feet of his host, who had walked out of the door on his way to work.

2

Mizprints

Isn't it amazing how you can say or write one thing and people hear directly the opposite of what you intended to communicate? At the close of a service a vicar announced: 'After the blessing the Bishop will leave and we will sing *Now thank we all our God.*'

Slip-ups in speech were highlighted by the Revd William Archibald Spooner who was born in 1844 and held the post of Warden at New College, Oxford, from 1903 to 1924. One day an event took place that changed the whole history of the English Language. During a service in the college chapel, Spooner arose and announced the next hymn as *Kinquering Kongs their titles take.*

That day the 'spoonerism' was born, the first of many attributed to this cleric. Others include:
'Let us toast the queer old dean.'
'You have tasted two whole worms and you must leave Oxford this afternoon by the town drain.'
'Give me a well boiled icycle.'
'It is roaring with pain outside.'
'I tried to stroke it, but it popped on its drawers and ran out of the room.'

Hi everyone!

Parishioners at St Mark's, Biggin Hill, were alarmed when they read their church magazine. An article about the Third World informed them that giving to a well known charity was 'equivalent to giving to poverty and dope.'

They were, however, soon reassured that their contributions would not go into the pockets of drug barons and that the article should have read 'equivalent to giving to poverty and hope.'

New copies of the magazine were later sent out.

Pot luck

'Women included their husbands and children in their pot-luck suppers.'

Converted cannibals, perhaps?

The end is nigh

'The vicar announced at the last meeting of the PCC that he was going to install a second font near the chancel steps, so that he could baptise babies at both ends.'

Dorking Parish church magazine

A generous offer

'The first Findon Valley Scout Group spent two hours collecting rubbish at the gallops in Findon

Valley. In return, each was given a portion of children and chips by Kentucky Fried Chicken food bar in Broadwater, Worthing.'

The Weston Evening Argus

Sin stroke

'Miss Hampshire…is friendly, likeable and easy to talk to. She has fine fair skin, which she admits ruefully comes out in a mass of freckles at the first hint of sin.'

Chichester Evening News

Bunyan's progress

'Next Wednesday in the church hall we shall see a set of slides on the progress of John Pilgrim's Bunyan.'

Donkey work

'The donkey failed to arrive for the Palm Sunday procession at St Peter's Church, Chippenham. The procession was led by the vicar, the Revd Jeremy Bray.'

An instant family

'A concert will be given in the Priory on Saturday at 7:30 by Joanne O'Fee and Caroline Jewson in aid of Cancer Research. Do come along—admission £2, children and old age pensioners will also be on sale.'

St Bee's Parish Church

Wild life

'The Women's Institute will hold their fortnightly lecture in St Mary's Hall. The topic will be "Country life" where Mrs Wills will show slides of some beautiful wild pants.'

Matlock Mercury

Money matters

'Fifteen churches have been closed in Dublin's city because of swindling congregations.'

Dublin Evening Herald

A great misnake

'The speaker told of her experience with a "bra constrictor".'

The Methodist Recorder

I can't find the rug

The Leicestershire Mercury carried this interesting quotation concerning the retirement of a local school mistress: 'At a presentation held in the village church, Mrs Jans was given a tea-set and a travelling rub by the vicar.'

Sinning lessons

'Miss Patricia Muddleton, qualified vice instructor, sang *Christian, dost thou see them?* on Sunday night.'

Yorkshire Post

A draining experience

'When you have emptied the teapot, please stand upside down in the sink.'

Notice in a church hall kitchen

Dead boring

'When you have finished reading this, please pass on.'

On a church magazine

A sticky spot

In a 1568 publication of the Bible is found 'Is there no treacle in Gilead?' instead of 'Is there no balm?'

Bless this house

A concert for the inmates of Pentonville Prison, with Harry Secombe as special guest, went well until he sang his famous rendition of *Bless this house* which includes the line 'Bless these walls so firm and stout, keeping want and trouble out.'

Socket and see

'The Electrical College of the Church in Wales will meet later this month to elect a new bishop for Swansea and Brecon.'

South Wales Evening Post

3

Wacky Weddings

Attempts at recreating the atmosphere where couples met have led to some interesting weddings. Like the couple who were married on a Concorde day trip to Cairo, or...

In with both feet

Deep sea diving fans Paul and Elaine Robinson said (or gurgled) 'I do' on the sea bed!

The British-born couple, now living in California, hired a boat to get them to their wedding twenty miles out at sea. The bride wore a skin diving suit and mask, as did most of the guests. Even the 'priest' was a diving buddy who got a special licence to conduct the ceremony this way.

I wonder if he was a Baptist minister?

Running into problems

Bruce Leone and Sharon Johnstone Bonora gave a new meaning to the phrase 'Get me to the church on time' — they took part in a marathon. The minister even agreed to perform the ceremony running backwards.

The couple obviously had no qualms about rushing into marriage. As they had both been brought together through marathon running, they considered it was only appropriate to marry while competing in the Seattle, Washington, race.

'WELL WHERE DID YOU DROP IT?'

Taking the plunge

A young Belgian couple, both keen members of their local subaqua club, hired the swimming pool in the small town of Kuurne for their wedding. They invited all their mates from the club, aqualungs in tow, for the event. The parish priest conducted the soggy ceremony, and as soon as their vows had been taken the bride and groom flung themselves in at the deep end, joined by the priest and guests, for their wedding photograph.

I heard that there wasn't a dry eye in the place.

The height of romance

When Wendy Stokes got married she wore white with a face to match.

She made her vows to Carl Bartoni, an escapologist, in an open sided, flower covered platform, 400 feet above Blackpool's Golden Mile. 'I do!' Wendy yelled. 'Now get me down from here.'

They were lowered to observation level where Father John Cayton performed a blessing ceremony, while down below, 15,000 bank holiday tourists joined the 15 choir boys in singing *All things bright and beautiful* as organ music was relayed over a loud-speaker system.

A good start

Bright spark Brian Delisle-Tarr suddenly realised during the wedding ceremony that he had forgotten to buy a ring. He left the church and rummaged around in his car tool box where he found a hose clip which he slipped onto Angela's finger, saying, 'It's amazing what useful items electricians carry around in their car boots'.

A piece of cake

The biggest wedding cake ever made was more than 40 feet in height. It contained 10,000 eggs, 352 pounds of flour and 550 pounds of butter.

Hymn number 999

When her car got stuck in the snow at Brighstone on the Isle of Wight, bride Helen Hayes was whisked to her wedding in a fire engine.

Bringing the house down

American fireman Ralph Deal chose to get married inside a burning building during a fire department training exercise. His 'old flame', Cheryl, looked wonderful in her fireproof uniform as the red-hot preacher led them in making their vows.

Bonanza

In Reno, queues of people come to get married at the church inside the Ponderosa Ranch, home of the television series Bonanza.

Ooops!

'The bride wore a long white dress that fell to the floor'

Newspaper misprint

In vogue

'The bride was gowned in white silk and lace. The colour scheme of the bridesmaids' gowns and flowers was punk.'

The Toronto Post

A big gamble

'It was announced today that the wedding would take place on 3rd July at St Mary's Church. Betting 9/4 against, 6-1, 10-1.'

Manchester Evening News

Putting the pressure on

Signing the register at a wedding, the best man had difficulty making his ball point pen work.

'Put you wieght on it', said the vicar.

He duly signed 'John Smith (10 stone 4 pounds).

Robot Rites

A Japanese couple had a yen to be married—by robot. They had attended the traditional weddings of their friends and, because they found the ceremonies 'yawn making', wanted something very different. And they got it!

The ultimate in hi-tech weddings featured a robot priest who told the bride and groom, through his built-in loudspeaker, 'One plus one is two.'

Who said marriage is old fashioned?

Dear dating company

'You might be interested to know that your computer managed to match me to an exceptional young man. He's handsome, intelligent and kind. We have exactly the same taste in music, politics, humour, hobbies, everything. He's perfect. There's only one snag...he's my brother.'

Letter to computer dating company

Getting your priorities right

'Nanyuki farmer seeks lady with tractor with view to companionship and possible marriage. Send picture of tractor. Little Wood. Box 132. Nanyuki.'

Advert in East Africa Standard

Worth a try

'Ugly, boring male (thirty-one) seeks beautiful, witty, rich young lady to prove that opposites attract.'

Lonely Hearts Column

Start again

When ranch owner Henry Joneson of Alberta saw an advert from a widow who 'wishes to start a new life...will relocate', he replied immediately.

He was shocked to discover that the advert had

been put in by Ada Wittermyer whose home was a Tennessee prison where she was serving life for murdering her third and fourth husbands.

Happy familes

After seventeen years of wedded bliss, a French restauranteur was told that owing to a clerical error, his father's name had been entered on his marriage certificate instead of his own. So until a court of law put matters right, his father was officially a bigamist, he was a bachelor, his sons were half-brothers, and his wife was his step-mother.

4

Dead Right

'POPE DIES AGAIN'

Newspaper headline

Not feeling well

'We are sorry to announce that Mr Albert Brown
has been quite unwell owing to his recent death and
is taking a short holiday to convalesce.'

Church Magazine

Short-lived

Scores of mourners attended the funeral of Mrs
Sadie Tuckey in Ontario, Canada, after she had
been accidentally knocked off her bicycle.

However, the mourners nearly died of shock as
the coffin was carried towards its final resting place.
Suddenly the lid opened and the body sat up in the

coffin. Mrs Tuckey had merely been stunned into a deep coma by the accident, and on awakening screamed. leapt out of the coffin with fright, and disappeared down the road straight into the path of a bus which killed her outright.

Bird brain

Ornithologist Marius Giraud was shot dead while doing bird impersonations.

'NEVER DID FIND OUT WHAT THAT BLIGHTER WAS'

Like a lamb to the slaughter

A man plumped for the hymn *Sheep may safely graze* at his funeral. He was a butcher.

Long lived

In 1562 Francois de Civille was dug up only six hours after his funeral because his brother had an intuition that he was still alive. The dead man revived and actually lived for another seventy years.

Francois eventually died at the age of 105, having caught a cold while serenading his lover all night long.

A voice from the grave

One of the latest fads in America is 'talking tombstones'. The manufacturer says that it cannot meet the current demand for these products.

They have a small speaker and a photo-electric cell built into them. Should a visitor approach the grave a tape recorded message is activated which announces something like: 'Hi! I was Fred Brown. I died at 10.25 on Friday 13th September, 1988. Thanks for coming to see me.'

It's the real thing

A Chinese interpreter translated 'Come alive with Pepsi' as 'Pepsi brings your relatives back from the dead.'

No other gods

Jesus said that many would come in his name saying that they were he, but people should not be deceived by them.

A classic example occurred in Naysmith's Square, Toronto, in September 1978 when Mrs Barbara Eastman was selling flowers.

She was suddenly approached by a man who announced, 'I am God. Could you direct me to the nearest church, please?'

Although somewhat surprised at his request, Mrs Eastman gave the necessary directions and watched in amazement at what happened next.

She later explained in court, 'When I had given him the directions, he took off his hat, said thank you, stepped out into the road, and was instantly killed by a tractor.'

Nobody at home

Police pulled up a macabre motorist who was seen driving down the motorway with a coffin strapped to the roof. The driver, theatre manager Neil Cooper, managed to convince them that there was 'no body' inside and that he was merely delivering a bizarre prop for his latest play *Shamrocks and Daffodils*. Mr Cooper said, 'They wanted me to open the coffin. They were dying to know what was inside.'

A fatal recipe

'Blend sugar, flour and salt. Add egg and milk. Cook until creamy in double boiler. Stir frequently, add rest of ingredients. Mix well and serve chilled. The funeral service will be held Thursday afternoon at two o'clock.'

Reedsburg Post

Rest in peace

'When you die, God takes care of you like your mother did when you were alive—only God doesn't yell at you all the time.'

Steve K. Aged eight

Surprise, surprise

Defending a decision to convert part of Shepton Mallet cemetery into a children's playground, the Bishop of Bath and Wells, Dr George Carey, explained to the Bristol Evening Post: 'Graveyards too often have a morbid atmosphere because people associate them with death.'

5

Hymns and Hers

One couple chose for their wedding hymn *Fight the good fight with all thy might*.

They were clearly starting off as they intended carrying on!

Hit on a sour note

A furious choir master beat up an old woman because she sang out of tune.

For years she had ignored his pleas to tone down the falsetto wailing during Sunday services, so he pounded her with a walking stick in the churchyard.

When charged, the Swedish choir-master told the police, 'Her singing was agony.'

Danger: choir at work

A notice in a church porch read: 'Next Sunday the choir will sing a cantata, after which the chapel will be closed for three weeks for repairs.'

Raising the roof

Three hundred and fifty singers from the Women's Institutes in Essex had an amazing escape at a music festival in Chelmsford.

They were told: 'Sing as you have never done before, raise the roof if you like'.

So they did—and part of it fell in.

The official reason for the collapse was vibrations made by workmen on another part of the roof. Some, however, were not convinced.

I've heard better choirs

One church pinned the sermon title 'What is hell like?' on their notice-board just above the comment 'Come and hear our choir'.

Bring-and-buy sale

'There will be a flower and vegetable competition as well as the baby competition already announced. All entries will become the property of the organising committee, who will sell them and give the money to charity.'

Church Magazine

Meet the cast

During the interval of a 1974 performance of the rock musical Godspell in London, members of the audience were invited up on stage to meet the cast.

One young lady left her seat, walked down the arcade outside and through the stage door. After climbing a flight of dark stairs she turned right and walked onto a brightly lit stage.

To her surprise, and that of everyone else, she found herself in the middle of the cast of *Pygmalion* at the theatre next door.

La Triviata

A special performance of *La Traviata* in honour of Pope John Paul II did not go quite as planned. Andrea Guiot, the leading soprano, had phoned the theatre to say that she had flu; the baritone, Julian Jiovenetti, rang saying that he was ill too, followed by a call from his wife thirty minutes later to say that he had died of a heart attack.

Hearing of Jiovenetti's death, contralto Helia Hezan broke down in hysterics and could not go on. Her understudy, Denise Montell, rushed to the theatre but was caught in a traffic jam.

Feeling the show might be jinxed, the theatre manager decided to cancel the performance, but leading tenor, Alexandre Mazota, would have none of it. 'Jinxed? Pah!' he said as he walked on the stage and fell through the trap door, breaking his leg.

Watch out!

A minister was handed a woman's watch that had been found in the aisle. He announced the find

42

from the pulpit and invited the owner to see him after the service. The final hymn was *Lord, her watch thy church is keeping*.

Turning up in force

'The service ended with the singing of the good old hymn *All police that on earth do dwell*.'

Toronto Post

Close friends

A retired priest who lived within earshot of St Edmund's Church, Huntstanton, decided to investigate when he heard some fierce playing on the church piano. He found an old tramp at the keyboard, going fifteen to the dozen, fortissimo, with his pack in the porch and his tea-tin on the literature table.

'Have you permission?' enquired Father Mather.

'Yes.'

'From whom?'

'From Jesus Christ' said the visitor indignantly.

'I don't get "yes" or "no" from him just like that,' replied Father Mather.

Without a second's hesitation the tramp retorted, 'Perhaps you don't know him as well as I do.'

To be or not to be

The fact that churches use different hymn books has caused some interesting problems.

A young man told the minister quite insistently that he wanted hymn number 774 at his wedding. Having failed to put him off, the minister announced the hymn during the ceremony. After the first verse, the organist had to stop playing because the congregation was in hysterics. The groom had failed to realise that the hymn he wanted was 774 in the Methodist Hymn Book, but the church he was married in used the 'Ancient & Modern' hymn book in which hymn number 774 is:

> 'Come O thou traveller unknown,
> Whom still I hold but cannot see.
> My company before me is gone,
> And I am left alone with thee.
> With thee all night I mean to stay
> And wrestle till the break of day'.

This may have been Wesley's favourite hymn, but it is not the best choice for a wedding. Or is it?

A right howl

NOW AVAILABLE
upon request for
special occasions
CHILDREN'S MINISTRY
JASPER THE SINGING DOG

Advert in American Christian magazine

6

Nun of That

'Most of the sketches were too long and rather lacked lustre. It was harmless family stuff which even the most devout nun would not object to her daughter seeing.'

Ipswich Evening Star

You're fired

Spanish priest, father Eliado Blanco, refused to attend the funeral of an eighty-seven-year-old widow, Felicita Gomez, because she had not been a church attender.

Relatives tried to drag him along to the funeral, so he pulled out a pistol and fired four shots, hitting one of them in the leg.

He was later arrested.

Pest control

'Environmental Protection Services. Professional control of rats, mice, insects and priests.'

Advert in Glasgow paper

Thou shalt not steal

While the Revd Edgar Dodson of Camden, North London, preached heartily on the eighth commandment 'Thou shalt not steal', his car was stolen from outside the church.

And...

While the Revd S Jones was chairing a meeting about the growing problem of burglary in his parish, two burglars rifled the bedroom of his vicarage in Merseyside and made off with the contents.

Lead us not into temptation

A New York lawyer, having driven round the court building for twenty minutes looking for a place to park, decided that he could wait no longer and parked in a 'no waiting' area. He left a note on the windscreen saying 'Drove round for twenty minutes; please forgive us our trespasses,' and put a five dollar bill in the note.

A little later he came out and went to his car to find his note and the five dollar bill still on the windscreen, along with a parking ticket and another note saying 'I have been a cop on this beat for twenty years. Lead us not into temptation.'

Eye eye eye

A man who confessed that he had unjustly spied on his neighbours was told to keep one eye shut for a hundred days as penance.

The man obliged.

Damsons in distress

One Derbyshire local preacher informed me of a very embarrassing experience he and his partner had on one preaching trip. As they had travelled quite a distance, tea had been arranged for them in a very 'posh' home. Being poor, simple believers, they did not know how to deal with the stones from the damsons that were served at tea-time, so they wrapped them up in their handkerchiefs. Later that evening, when the service was well under way, the young man pulled his handkerchief out of his pocket, scattering the stones over the top of the pulpit and showering the congregation.

Let us...

A couple who had recently moved to a new area decided to visit the local parish church. Although they had previously attended an evangelical Anglican church, the woman was caught off guard as she walked along the isle. Another lady was genuflecting. As she had to stop, she tripped over the woman, both of them ending up flat on their faces in the centre of the church.

Young mothers

As the vicar concluded the Sunday morning service, he suddenly remembered the new Young Mothers' Group his wife was starting that week.

Without thinking he announced 'If any of the young women in our church want to become young mothers, come and see me in the vestry at the close of the service.'

Thou shalt not murder

'A missionary charged with killing her husband during an argument over who had saved more souls has been acquitted of murder by a judge who accepted her plea of self-defence.'

Vancouver Sun

Getting into bad habits

A mad monk took his anger out on a town in a ten-ton truck.

The brother, a Carthusian monk from a monastery near Horsham, whacked a bollard, rammed a metal lamppost, and was only stopped when he hit a road sign.

Although he had taken a vow of silence, he told police that he had become angry because he couldn't find a phone box that worked to call a relative.

'OH NO NOT ANOTHER ONE'

Part one

A new convert wrote a letter to the Inland Revenue saying 'I can't sleep at night so I am enclosing £100 I forgot to declare.

PS   If I still can't sleep I will send the rest.'

Cardinal Sin

The head of the Roman Catholic Church in the Philippines is called Cardinal Sin.

Mistaken identity

A vicar who spent Lent in a chicken wire cage to get a Russian 'priest' freed from jail has discovered that the man is a tramp.

The Revd Dick Rodgers campaigned for ten years with gruelling hunger strikes for dissident Vasily Shipilov.

Finally Shipilov was freed after forty-five years in Soviet labour camps.

But yesterday, after meeting him for the first time in Moscow, Mr Rodgers revealed that Shipilov never was a priest—and was first jailed for vagrancy.

And the vicar of Shenley, Birmingham, admitted he felt 'embarrassed'. He spent Lent eating a prison camp diet at a London church.

A clerical error

'After evensong on April 24th we made presenta-
tions to Bill and Patience Ofield on their Golden
Wedding anniversary. We had a larger congregation
than usual and everyone enjoyed the service despite
the fact that the Rector fell out of the pulpit.'

St Mary the Virgin

Just call me father

A Portuguese man living in Brazil during the fif-
teenth century was convicted after it was discovered
that he was the father of two hundred and ninety-
nine children by fifty-nine different women, including his own mother, five of his sisters, twenty-nine
adopted daughters and three of his slaves.

The fact that Father Fernando de Coster was the
local priest may have influenced the judge's
decision.

51

I confess

Because the priest was rather deaf, the parishioners were asked to write their sins on a piece of paper and pass it over in the confessional.

This worked well until one woman passed him a slip bearing the message: '$\frac{1}{2}$lb tea, $\frac{1}{2}$lb butter, 2lb sugar, $\frac{1}{2}$lb cheese.'

When it was passed back, the absent minded woman was overcome with acute embarrassment at the list of sins she had left with her grocer!

Let there be light

The church business meeting moved to item five on the agenda. It read 'Purchase of candelabra.'

One long-standing member stood up—a man who occasionally got hold of the wrong end of the stick.

'I'm against this idea,' he declared. 'For one thing we have just overhauled the organ. For another thing, no one in the church can play the candelabra. In any case, if we have any spare funds we should concentrate on improving the lighting in the church.'

Every little helps

'The minister is going on holiday next Saturday. Please return all missionary boxes by Friday evening at the latest.'

From a church news sheet

7

Nothing to Hide

From the day that Adam made fig leaves to cover himself in the garden, nudity has been a source of embarrassment.

For example, Pope Paul IV ordered Michelangelo to paint clothes on all the naked bodies on the Sistine Chapel in Rome.

Excuses

When no one answered the front door, the vicar, knowing that somebody was at home, left his visiting card with the scripture Revelation 3:20 written on the back: 'Behold I stand at the door and knock; if any one hears my voice and opens the door, I will come in.'

Next Sunday when people were leaving the church, a lady handed him her own card on which she had written: 'Genesis 3:10— "I heard the sound of thee in the garden, and I was afraid, because I was naked; and hid myself."'

Bare Methodists

A notice was seen in a train window: 'Reserved for
Bare Methodists.'
   Apparently a group of Methodists from Bare had
reserved the seats for their day out to the seaside.

All change

'The ladies of St Martin's have discarded clothing of
all kinds. Call at 152 North Street for inspection.
Mrs Freeman will be willing to oblige you in any way
she can.'

Caught with his trousers on

The 1820 Trust Deed of a Kent non-conformist chapel reads 'In no circumstances shall a preacher who wears trousers ever be allowed to occupy a pulpit.'

Nothing between us

The prime red-face award must go to the Revd J Fellers of Shrieveport, Louisiana, who was confronted on entering his church by a woman kneeling naked at the altar.

When he questioned her behaviour she replied 'Minister, I didn't mean to embarrass you. I didn't want anything between me and the Lord.'

After this encounter, the woman dressed and promptly left.

'Strange things happen in the ministry,' said Fellers, 'but they don't prepare you for this.'

Bizarre baptisms

A sheet had been erected behind the baptistry in a small Welsh chapel so that the two skinny male candidates could get changed while the minister baptised a rather large female candidate.

Everything went well, until fear struck the woman's heart as the minister attempted to immerse her. Striking out in an attempt to avoid being dunked, she grabbed hold of the sheet which fell down and revealed the two unclad males who duly jumped into the baptismal pool to cover their embarrassment.

8

A Grave Mistake

This interesting sign was seen in a Pennsylvanian cemetery: 'Persons are prohibited from picking flowers from any but their own grave.'

Tactless tombstones

Here lies the body of SARAH, wife of John Hayes,
Who died on 24th March 1823 AD aged 42 years.
The Lord giveth and the Lord taketh away.
Blessed be the name of the Lord.

Gravestone in Kent

Underneath this pile of stones
Lies all that's left of Sally Jones.
Her name was Briggs, it was not Jones,
But Jones was used to rhyme with stones.

Gravestone in New York

Thomas Alleyn and his Two Wives, ob 1650
Death here have advantage of life I spye
One husband with two wives at once may lye

Gravestone in Norfolk

Tombstone of a hypochondriac

'I told you I was sick'

Last requests

A musician passed away, having left strict orders that his flute was to be buried with him.

'What did you make of that?' a friend asked the widow.

'It's a blessing he didn't play the piano,' she replied.

Ashes to ashes

A New York funeral parlour was banned from releasing a doctor's ashes to his widow. She had been cut out of her husband's will and was threatening to fix him once and for all by flushing them down the lavatory.

ANY CLOSER
AND HE GETS
IT!

As well as can be expected

'Mr Bromsgrove suffered a stroke on 24th November 1980, but with the loving care of his family and his kind and efficient nurse, he never fully recovered.'

I feel like a king

When ill, Ethiopian Emperor Menelik II regularly ate a few pages of the Bible to restore his health. Unfortunately he died in 1913 after eating the entire book of Kings.

Restaurant closed

'Mrs Freda Brown, seventy-nine, dined this week at her home. Service and cremation will be held next Thursday at 2.00pm.'

Accrington Weekly

Famous last words

During a battle in the American civil war, General John Sedgewick squinted at the enemy guns and pronounced: 'They couldn't hit an elephant at that range.'

These were his very last words before the very same guns blasted him to death.

'I'm getting better.'

The final words of D H Lawrence in 1930

'Good Night.'

Byron's last words

'I'm looking for a loophole.'

W C Fields' death-bed reply, when asked why he was reading the Bible

Dead close

'Mr Douglas Gordon, aged fifty-six, was taken to hospital in Nottingham last night after he had been seen to move in a coffin at an undertaker's mortuary. He was given emergency treatment at the hospital after it had been confirmed that he was still alive.'

The Times

Going out in style

Mrs Sandra West, a Texan millionairess who died in March 1977, requested that she be buried in a lace nightdress in her favourite Ferrari car.

A court hearing granted her wish and on 19 May the extraordinary burial took place.

All hands on deck

'Due to industrial action, the cemetery will be run by a skeleton staff.'

Seen outside a cemetery

The final curtain

A man from Cumnor, Oxfordshire, who had always wanted to be an actor, left his skull to the Royal Shakespeare Company for use in productions of *Hamlet*.

A spokesman for the theatre company said, 'We have no plans to stage *Hamlet* in the near future.'

9

Tee-Total-Hic-Ism

Water into wine

A visiting preacher concluded his fiery discourse on teetotalism and the demon drink with the solemn statement: 'I hope the time will come when all liquor will be poured into the river.'

To his dismay, the closing hymn was then announced: *Shall we gather at the river?*

Thanks

A vicar had a friend who was noted for his love of cherry brandy. One day the cleric asked him if he could have a bottle. The friend wryly replied, 'Only on one condition, and that is that you are prepared to publish the fact in the church magazine.'

'Certainly', said the vicar. 'If you turn to the *Thanks* column in the next magazine, you will find my word of thanks.'

The next month, sure enough, it was there:

'We thank our kind friend very much for his gift of cherries, and particularly for the spirit in which they were sent.'

Cheese and wine party

The Revd Dennis Caddy got more than he bargained for when he left a trail of cheese in the church vestry to lure mice into the traps he had put down. The mice retaliated with a raid on his stock of communion wine.

Dennis, Rector of St Margaret's Church in Corsley, Wiltshire, said, 'They nibbled through the tops and sipped the stuff straight from the bottles. They had opened six bottles before they were found out and we had to throw them all away.'

A day off

Magistrates in Kent queried the application to sell intoxicating liquor at the first anniversary celebration of a temperance club.

Hic!

'The deacons' meeting on Thursday will be gin with a prayer.'

Walton Baptist Church newsletter

10

Words of Wisdom

Part-time jobs available

When Pope John XXIII was asked how many people worked in the Vatican, he replied, 'Oh, about half of them.'

Good news for the poor

'It is well known that I have always welcomed the poor to my church,' a vicar declared. 'Looking at the collection, I see they have come.'

Excellent service

'Unlike the Post Office, we have two collections every Sunday.'

On a church notice board

Hear my prayer

Pastor Graham Gardiner, who preaches to 200 vacant seats each Sunday, put a hoarding outside his Nottinghamshire Baptist church carrying the message: 'Lonely preacher requires congregation. Apply within.'

RSVP

'When you were born your mother brought you here. When you were married your wife brought you here. When you die your friends will bring you here. Why not try coming on your own sometimes?'
St Chad's Magazine

Saving Soles

'Shoe Repairs', a shop in Poole, Dorset, offered 'new soles for old' when customers called in—and a chat about the Lord.

Divine guidance

'There will be a procession next Sunday afternoon in the grounds of the monastery, but if it rains in the afternoon the procession will take place in the morning.'
Hampshire parish magazine

The sound of silence

'We regret to announce that the Ladies Happy Hour are in debt following their recent sponsored silence.'

Pardon?

An elderly man was teaching on door to door visitation. The subsequent discussion related to problems that might arise. A Nigerian man sitting near the back of the class asked a question. Unable to understand him, the speaker asked him to raise his voice. The man spoke up and asked the question again. However, after three times the lecturer couldn't understand him, and in despair he asked some students nearby to repeat the man's question.

It was: 'What do you do if you go to a door and a deaf person answers it?'

The bear essentials

Students at a British Bible college were watching a film about the life of President Roosevelt. One of them was very engrossed in the film, but he had to leave the TV lounge before the end to receive a phone call. Later, after the film had finished, he came back into the room and asked one of the students what had happened. In a jocular mood, one of them said, 'You know Roosevelt was given a present of a stuffed bear?'

'Yes,' the student replied eagerly.

'Well, right at the end of the film, as he sat in his office writing on his desk, the bear actually fell on him and killed him.'

The next day, the student was preaching in a church on the shortness of life. 'I don't care who you are and I don't care how important you are,' he declared.' Your life is short and can end at any moment. Even someone as great as President Roosevelt had no idea that his life would end when that stuffed bear fell on him.'

All welcome

Many American churches advertise their forthcoming sermon titles on notice boards outside the building. The following are some of the worst of the bunch.

'Seek a spiritual fix in '86'

'We didn't know who you was'

'Up to your neck in whale puke'

'Meet Mr Happiness'

'Do I have to wear a bun in my hair? (Matthew 5:28)'

'A problem of denial—do you really love God, or are there roosters in your life?'

'A soul on an unbroken spinnet'

'The 1986 Lenten Christian education series—Do's and don'ts on real estate'

11

Give Us a Break

Much interest was recently raised by the Sunday Trading Bill. However, it has been an issue in America for many years.

* In Opal, Wyoming, any woman weighing over 200 pounds cannot ride a horse in public on Sundays.

* In Idanha, Oregon, eating watermelon is banned on Sundays.

* On Sundays using a yo-yo is banned in Studley, Virginia.

* Turtle races are banned in Slaughet, Louisiana, on the 'Sabbath'.

* In Leona, Texas, the law states that a woman must be fully dressed before she is assisted by firemen during a fire on Sunday.

* In Gilman, Connecticut, anyone caught slurping soup in public on Sundays is liable to arrest and a $5 fine.

* Lingerie cannot be hung on the clothes-line in Toomborro, Georgia, on Sundays unless the items are hidden by a screen or fence.

12

In For a Service

Although sincere, the old rector was sometimes absent-minded. One Sunday during evensong, as the congregation reached the creed, everything went silent. The curate went across and touched the rector gently on the arm, whispering in his ear, 'I believe in God, sir.'

'So do I,' replied the rector with a smile on his face, 'So do I.'

Deadly service

The church service was far too long for Billy, aged seven. He looked round for interesting distractions. 'What's that?' he asked, pointing to some names on the Roll of Honour affixed to the wall.

'Those are people who died in the Services', whispered his mother.

'Oh', said Billy. 'Did they die in the morning or the evening services?'

High flying

During a church service the speaker from the Missionary Aviation Fellowship, an organisation which flies missionaries around the world, explained that there was to be a change in leadership in the organisation and asked for a spirit of peace and unity to reign among the new leaders.

When the church had a time of prayer, an old lady stood up and said, 'Lord Jesus, we do pray for the aviations and we do ask that you will give them concord.'

Idi Amen

Major evangelistic crusades attract crowds of thousands, especially in third world countries. At one crusade in Uganda, Idi Amin flew over in his helicopter and assumed that it was a welcoming party for one of his major political rallies. He ordered the helicopter to land and proceeded to walk onto the platform. Only then did he realise his mistake. But he continued to shake hands with the ministers, addressed the crowd and then returned to his waiting helicopter which whisked him off to those awaiting his political speech—a much smaller congregation.

A good sermon

A young man who was hoping to be a preacher met a man who had been preaching for many years who told him that a good sermon had three main requirements: it needed to be moving, soothing and satisfying.

Some months later he met the same man, who asked him, 'Do you think your sermons have the necessary requirements?'

'Well, I think they must have,' he said. 'I was preaching at a church, and undoubtedly my sermon was moving because as I preached several people got up and walked out. It was soothing because I noticed that a number of them were asleep, and I know they were satisfied because they never asked me again.'

Beware all who enter

'Danger—Services'

*Sign left by builders outside
an Anglican church in Esher*

Confirmation

'The vicar reported an increased number of communicants during the year. He also stated that the Death Watch Beetle had been confirmed in the church.'

Seaton parish magazine

Communion

When a Baptist Church in Nottingham ran out of the non-alcoholic blackcurrant juice they used at communion services, the resourceful server improvised by diluting some blackcurrant jelly and pouring it into the individual cups. The inevitable happened, and when the congregation stood to drink simultaneously they found that the jelly had set in the cups.

What you might call separating the 'juice' from the gentiles!

A short service

Corcuetos Cathedral, Spain, took ninety years to build and collapsed in 1625 on the day it was finished.

Baptism

Seeking to dispel any idea that there was something special about the water used for the baptismal service, the minister said, 'There's nothing magical about this water. It's the same water that we shall make the coffee with later.'

Christening

A most unorthodox christening event took place in the nineteenth century at a church in Great Yarmouth. A child was christened as a boy, but three weeks later he was brought back to be 'rechristened' as 'he' was actually a girl.

Strange names

Ministers have been faced with some interesting and unusual names that parents have decided to give their children. After all, who would have named John Wayne 'Marion', or the wrestler 'Big Daddy' Shirley Crabtree? One parent went as far as to name his child after the entire Manchester United football team, and another called his son 'Cigar Stubbs'. One poor man was even called 'Francis Mary'. He was rarely teased, however, being captain of the local Rugby team.

Telephone directories make fascinating reading when it comes to surnames. The San Francisco issue has a Karl Marx, four James Bonds and five Goldfingers. Love outnumbers Lust by seventy-three to three, and there are thirty-six Hammers, four Nails, two Tacks, five Bolts and one Nutt.

The New York Phone directory has a Mona Lisa Gooseberry, an Oscar Asparagus and a Lizzie Izabitchie.

In Massachussetts there is a Mr Preserved Fish, a Preserved Fish Jr, and a Mr and Mrs Silver who gave their son the initials I O.

13

Sunday Skool

A small boy asked his mother for a cucumber to take to Sunday School. Although she was slightly puzzled at his request, his mother complied.

Later that day, when she asked him what the cucumber had been used for, he confessed, 'Sorry, Mum, I got it wrong. We were supposed to bring a newcomer.'

What's his name?

A woman asked her son what he had done at school.

'We visited a church today and saw a vicar baptising a baby,' he replied.

'Oh, what did he say?' the woman asked.

'I baptise you in the name of the Father, Son and overgoes.'

'You mean the Holy Ghost, don't you?' she questioned.

'No I don't' he replied. 'I mean overgoes because it was then that he threw water over the baby.'

A surprise present

At the town carol service in Arundel cathedral, the bishop gathered the children round the crib and told them the story of the three wise men. To make sure they had all the details crystal clear he then asked them a few questions.

'Now, who can tell me what gifts the wise men gave to the baby Jesus?' he asked.

A little voice piped up confidently, 'Gold, Frankenstein and myrrh.'

Sparks will fly

'What are standards?' a preacher sternly enquired of his young people's group on the Sunday before bonfire night.

'Fireworks, sir', one young boy cheekily replied.

In active service

After a Sunday School teacher had given a lesson on the twelve disciples, she gave pencils to the children and asked them to draw the twelve. One child drew three cars and a man standing in front.

'What's that?' asked the teacher.

'Matthew,' the child replied. 'You said he was a collector of taxis.'

Don't let him out

A little girl who was used to Anglican services was taken to another church where the fiery minister vigorously waved his arms and banged on the pulpit as he preached.

After a while she whispered to her father in a frightened voice, 'What will we do if he gets out?'

Travelling companions

A Sunday school teacher told the story of the flight into Egypt and then asked the children to draw the scene. One little girl drew a splendid picture of Mary and Jesus on the donkey, with Joseph beside them and a large insect accompanying them.

When asked what the insect was, she replied 'You said "Take the young child and flea into Egypt."'

Just in time for tea

Some children were performing a nativity play and had got as far as the point when the inn-keeper said to Mary, 'You cannot come in, there is no room.' The little 'inn-keeper' spontaneously added, 'Oh, come in for a cup of tea, but then you must go.'

Free worship

A man from Leicester took his grandson to church for the first time. The lad was surprised when the collection plate came round. 'You don't have to pay for me, Grandad,' he whispered. 'I'm not five yet.'

Walkies

An American author has written a book entitled 'Perfect Pets—Obedient Children.'

She wrote the book after she noticed that Biblical principles could be used for raising children and training animals. The book was originally called *Dominion over Rover*. As she wrote in the introduction:

'The book is geared to the enlightenment of individuals wishing to understand and train their dogs with a high degree of success and a minimal amount of confusion using principles and common sense....I truly believe that when using Biblical principles for training children or handling animals that you cannot fail. I have come to the conclusion that, with God, all things are relative. One thing complements another. The same holds true in the remarkable similarity in training animals and raising obedient children. Over the years, I have discovered that the two inevitably share the same home.'

The author runs a company called 'Christian Canine Concept' and travels around America sharing her experiences at public and home meetings.

Hand it to him

A zealous Sunday school teacher had been telling her little group of children how they must try to be 'like God' in all they did.

Later that day the mother of one of the children noticed that her small son was doing everything with his left hand, although he was right handed. When she asked him about this he replied, 'I'm trying to be like God.'

'But why are you doing everything with your left hand?' his mother further enquired.

'Well, God must be left handed,' the child replied innocently, 'because Jesus sits on his right hand.'

Dead right

The Sunday school teacher expected Jimmy, aged five, to reply 'a Christian' when she asked him the question, 'what do you have to be to go to heaven?' However, his reply stunned her: 'You have to be dead.'

14

Classic Comments—All From Children

'Joan of Arc was Noah's wife.'

'A layman is someone who lays in bed on Sunday mornings.'

'My father is a civil serpent.'

'When a woman has many husbands it is called Pollyanna.'

'When a man is married to one woman it is called monotony.'

'Jacob had a brother called See-saw.'

'Insects is burned in some churches.'

'If God rested on the seventh day, why do we have to go to Sunday school?'

'The Agnus Dei is a woman composer of music.'

'An epistle is the wife of an apostle.'

'The fast days are the days when you have to eat in a hurry.'

'Adultery is the sin of saying you're older than you really are.'

'The people of Lystra did not like Paul's message, so he got stoned.'

'I wish my dad was a pastor so he only had to work one day a week.'

'A bishop wears a meter on his head.' (Obviously to increase the offerings.)

Teacher: 'What did Jesus say to the girl whom he brought back to life?'
Child: 'Wake up! Your dinner's ready!'

'Jesus spoke in Aromatic.'

'I will make you vicious old men.' (I will make you fishers of men.)

'Apple Farmer let me be yours and yours alone.'

'David fought the Philadelphian Giants.'

'Mary and Joseph could not stay at the inn as it was Christmas and it was full up.'

15

Thought For The Day

(Courtesy of the Authorised Version.)

Courage best

'When the brethren heard of us, they came to meet us as far as Appii Forum and the three taverns; whom when Paul saw he thanked God and took courage.'

Acts 28:15

Where's the milkman?

'And he said unto her, "Give me I pray thee a little water to drink, for I am thirsty." And she opened a bottle of milk.'

Judges 4:19

Making an ass of yourself

'And he spake to his sons, saying, "Saddle me the ass." And they saddled him.'

1 Kings 13:27

16

Christmas Crackers

Mr Terence Dunklin from Oxford justified tearing the fixtures and fittings from his walls, the phone from its socket, wrenching the bath from its pipes, throwing his TV and hi-fi through his front window and destroying his bedroom suite, saying: 'I was shocked by the over-commercialism of Christmas.'

X-mas

In 1647 Christmas was abolished by the English Parliament.

What a boar

Boar's head used to be the popular Christmas treat before the advent of turkey, and mince pies were originally made from a mixture of ox tongue, chicken, egg, sugar, raisins, lemon, orange peel and various spices.

Apply now

'Come to church this Sunday and avoid the Christmas rush.'

Birmingham church's November notice

A tall story

The tallest Christmas tree erected in Britain was the 85 feet 3¼ inch spruce from Norway, erected for the Canterbury cathedral appeal on London's South Bank on 20th November 1975.

The world's tallest Christmas tree was a 221 feet Douglas fir erected at Northgate shopping centre, Seattle, in 1950.

30,000 unexpected guests

A live Christmas tree is home for about 30,000 creepy crawlies, including midges, fleas, lice, spiders and beetles. Most of them die when it is brought indoors.

Saint Nic

St Nicholas, who has become better known as Father Christmas, is actually the patron saint of thieves, virgins and Russia.

Where's the chimney?

Father Christmas, alias Stephen Perks, crept inside a cupboard to hide from the youngsters at a school where his wife worked. He intended it to be a Christmas surprise for her. However, the self-locking door imprisoned him. Fortunately there was a telephone in the cupboard and when he had eventually convinced the operator that his story was true, someone was sent to release him.

There's snow business like show business

They say that money can't buy everything, but Dynasty producer Aaron Spelling ordered several lorry loads of snow to be specially delivered to his home on Christmas Eve, so that his children woke up to a white Christmas.

A happy ending

During Christmas 1977, John Helms, a poverty stricken young artist in New York, decided that life was no longer worth living and that he would kill himself.

He took a lift to the eighty-sixth floor of the Empire State Building, more than 1,000 feet up, and jumped.

Half an hour later he came round to find himself on a thirty inch ledge on the eighty-fifth floor, where strong winds had blown him. He knocked on the window of a television station and crawled in.

Bill Stockman, who was working there at the time, said 'I couldn't believe it. You don't see a lot of guys coming in through the window of the eighty-fifth floor. I poured myself a stiff drink.'

Helms found that Christmas was not such a bad time as hundreds of families phoned him up, offering him a home for the holidays.

17

Archbishop Travolta

During a visit to New York a former Archbishop of Canterbury was met by a group of newspaper reporters anxious for an interesting story. 'Did his Grace plan to visit any of New York's famous night clubs during his stay?' they asked.

'Are there any nightclubs in New York?' the Archbishop wryly replied.

To his horror, the headlines in all the major newspapers the next day read 'Archbishop's first question on arrival: "ARE THERE ANY NIGHTCLUBS IN NEW YORK?"'

Wrong shade

A well known bishop was speaking to a group of girls on the use of cosmetics.

'The more experience I have with lipstick,' he pronounced, 'the more distasteful I find it.'

Highway patrol

In 1850 The Gentleman's Magazine explained that Bishop Raphoe had died after being taken mysteriously ill on Hounslow Heath with 'an inflammation of the bowels'.

This story was, however, invented as a cover-up to save the Church's face. It was a cryptic reference to the Bishop's part-time occupation as a highwayman. He had, in fact, been shot and killed by one of his intended victims while carrying out a robbery on Hounslow Heath.

A right crook

A young boy sitting near the front at a confirmation service was intrigued by the shepherd's crook which the bishop carried.

At Sunday school the following week he was asked to write about the confirmation. 'Last Sunday I sat near the bishop,' he wrote. 'Now I know what a real crook looks like.'

Pontificating

Some invalids were taken to receive a blessing from the Pope. One of the doctors decided to settle in an empty wheel-chair for a rest. However, a well-meaning nun spotted him and immediately wheeled him, despite his protests, to the end of the line for an audience with the Pontiff.

The Pope made the sign of the cross and blessed

Doctor Laverick who instantly rose to his feet to explain the mistake. There was a chorus of gasps from the assembled congregation, and a group of nuns exclaimed, 'It's a miracle.'

Doctor Laverick commented 'The Pope read my identity badge, then looked at me in a strange way.'

Oh dear, what can the matter be?

Just before a service at St Albans cathedral, the Bishops of St Albans, Bedford and Hertford got locked in the upstairs vestry. They raised the alarm—and a verger walked down the aisle with a ladder as the congregation rolled with laughter in the pews.

The bishops, however, decided that it would be undignified to use the ladder and waited fifteen minutes for the door to be freed before entering the church to rousing applause.

What was her name?

A bishop decided he would like to hear how well his new curate preached, so he slipped into the back of the church to hear him. The curate stood up and his opening words were, 'I have spent the most enjoyable years of my life in the arms of another man's wife.' He then proceeded to preach about his own mother.

Impressed at the curate's opening gambit, the bishop, who was known to be quite absent-minded, decided he too would use it in the cathedral on

Sunday morning. He stood up and proclaimed, 'I have spent the happiest years of my life in the arms of another man's wife...Oh, now, what was her name again?'

18

Heavens Above

No entry

Engraved above the door of a church in Stafford is the quotation: 'This is the gate of heaven. Enter you all by this door.'

However, a notice has been pinned to the door saying: 'This door is kept locked because of draughts. Please use the back entrance.'

Casablanca

'It must have been the most melodramatic farewell to be filmed since Bogart said goodbye to Bergman in *Casablanca*, as the Scotland World Cup squad at Hampden last night waved farewell to over 35,000 hell-wishers.'

The Edinburgh Evening News

A head start

Arriving home from school, where they had been discussing the subject of death, a boy questioned his parents further on the subject. Trying to get across some spiritual truth about eternal life, his father commented, 'Only the body is buried.' Before he could say any more about where the soul went, his son inquisitively said, 'What do they do with the head?'

The final judgement

The vicar was hot and strong on the subject of heaven and hell. However, one chap at the back of the church had fallen asleep.

Noticing him, the vicar said, 'All those who want to go to heaven stand on your feet!' at which the entire congregation stood up, except for this one man who continued to sleep.

With a fiery thump on the pulpit, the vicar cried, 'All those who want to go to hell stand on your feet!'

Awakened by the thump on the pulpit, the man jumped to his feet. After a moment's pause he said, looking around him, 'Well, Vicar, I don't know what's on offer, but it looks as if you and I are the only ones who want it.'

Gnashing of teeth

A preacher waxing eloquent in his sermon on 'hell-fire', exclaimed, 'There will be weeping and gnashing of teeth there.'

'I haven't got any teeth.' One old man at the back of the hall retorted.

'Teeth will be provided,' the preacher replied.

One way!

Billy Graham was visiting an American town and needed to ask a young lad the way to the post office.

Dr Graham thanked the boy for his directions and added, 'If you come to the Baptist church this evening, you can hear me telling everyone how to get to heaven.'

'I don't think I'll be there,' the boy replied. 'You don't even know the way to the post office.'